PACKRAFTING

A BEGINNER'S GUIDE

CHRIS SCOTT

FERNHURST
BOOKS

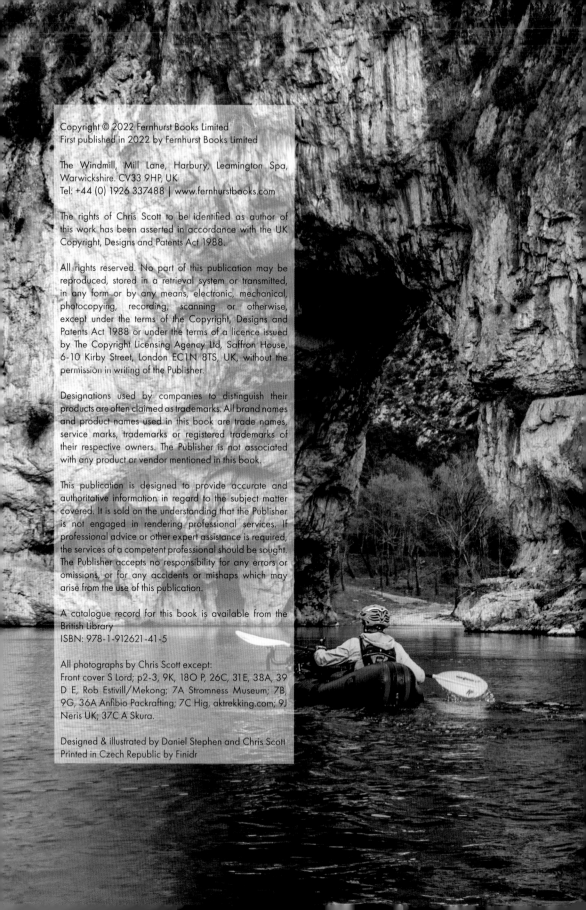

A catalogue record for this book is available from the
British Library
ISBN: 978-1-912621-41-5

All photographs by Chris Scott except:
Front cover S Lord; p2-3, 9K, 18O P, 26C, 31E, 38A, 39
D E, Rob Estivill/Mekong; 7A Stromness Museum; 7B,
9G, 36A Anfibio Packrafting; 7C Hig, aktrekking.com; 9J
Neris UK; 37C A Skura.

Designed & illustrated by Daniel Stephen and Chris Scott
Printed in Czech Republic by Finidr

INTRODUCTION

If you enjoy exploring wild places, a packraft will be a game changer. A boat that's genuinely portable yet robust and easy to paddle transforms the way you approach outdoor adventures. The clue's in the name: you can pack up your raft in minutes, hike for hours or days, then reinflate effortlessly at the water's edge before paddling onwards. On calm water you don't need any special skills, but as with all paddle boats, it's important to understand the risks, especially on fast-flowing rivers and exposed crossings.

The picture left was taken at the start of an 80-mile adventure along a wild river in the Australian outback. Dropped off at a remote airstrip, we carried everything we needed for a week, a journey only made viable with packrafts. Nearer home, the **Scottish Highlands** are where packrafting adventures jump off the map. Obscure lochs and meandering rivers are no longer obstacles but new byways, enabling easy or challenging routes limited only by your imagination.

At a glance, a 3-kilo packraft may resemble a cheap vinyl beach toy, but it's the durable fabric and hand-made construction that puts these boats in a class of their own. This enables higher pressures: the key to a responsive boat and an enjoyable paddling experience which won't end with a hiss on brushing past a twig. There are some compromises – if you're hoping for a nippy glorified kayak, you may be disappointed. On flat water packrafts are relatively slow and easily affected by winds. Above all, it's the places you can access which sets packrafts apart.

Paddling is also a low-impact way of enjoying the outdoors. Combining walking and even cycling are all part of getting the most from your lightweight boat. *Packrafting: A Beginner's Guide* is crammed with ideas, hard-won knowledge, tips and safety advice to show you how to get started. Once you've embraced the full potential of packrafting, you'll look at the outdoors with completely new eyes.

Chris Scott
inflatablekayaksandpackrafts.com

ABOUT PACKRAFTS

PACKRAFTS & PACKBOATS

In the world of paddle boats the **packraft** occupies a tiny enthusiasts' niche. Though it's how I came to it, the crossover between inflatable kayaks (IK) is slim because, while they're as convenient to store and transport, the lightest decent IK weighs three or four times more than a packraft.

And compared to IK users, packrafters are a different bunch too: more active and maybe even adventurous, they're more likely to have come from a backpacking or mountain biking background, than kayaking or canoeing.

At first sight a packraft on the water is not so arresting: a rotund mini-raft that doesn't so much knife through the water as bob along in the breeze. What does capture the imagination is seeing the same boat easily carried under one arm, or rolled up and lashed to a backpack or around a paddle shaft in a couple of minutes before the user heads off into the wilds on foot or by bike.

A PACKRAFT FOR YOU

Compared to other paddle sports, packrafting is still very much a cottage industry so you're unlikely to see one, far less a selection of brands at an outdoor sports outlet. Prices start **from just £330/€400**, although **double that** widens your options greatly. In the end it might just be down to colour, price and availability.

The best-known brands in North America are **Alpacka** who led the way, and **Kokopelli** (now China-made). In Europe you'll find both, as well as **Anfibio** in Germany (Chinese-made), Russian-made **Nortik**, and unapologetically all-Chinese and widely distributed **MRS**. Other popular brands include French-made **Mekong**, Ukrainian **Neris** distributed in Europe and a couple of other East European brands. In the US, Aire, Advanced Elements and NRS also make at least one packraft.

Online, unbranded bargains on Alibaba can be tempting – are they unbranded 'left-overs' or shoddy knock-offs? **Chinese manufacture** can be a minefield but the branded, Chinese-made packrafts I've owned or tried easily match the quality of my old Alpackas. It's just a packraft made of carefully hand-assembled sections of fabric that you can even make yourself (p8).

PACKRAFTING GLOSSARY

Bow/Stern: Front/back ends of a boat.
Cockpit: Where you sit, usually open.
Deck: Optional cover to keep water out.
Hardshell: Hard plastic kayak/canoe.
IK: Inflatable kayak.
PFD: Personal flotation device ('lifejacket').
Portage: Carrying boat round an obstacle.
Psi: pounds/inch2. 14.5psi = 1 bar

Put-in/Take-out: River entry/exit points.
Rapid: 'Whitewater' (more on p16).
Skeg: aka: tracking fin.
TPU: Thermoplastic polyurethane; heat weldable PU-coated nylon fabric. **PVC** is an alternative.
TiZip: Popular brand of airtight zippers.
Trim: Bow-to-stern level. Horizontal is best.
Yawing: The normal side-to-side movement.

THE INVENTION OF PACKRAFTING

The idea for a modern packable raft followed the invention of 'Mackintosh' rubberised canvas. In the 1840s Peter Halkett, an enterprising British naval officer, produced a 'marine contrivance' (A) designed to aid exploration of the Canadian Arctic. A century ahead of his time, his 3.4-kilo, four-chamber raft doubled as a waterproof cloak and though it failed commercially, Halkett clearly had a contemporary, 'Backpacking Light' mentality towards multi-functional gear.

Larger rubberised canvas vessels ensued, but portable rafts sank into a century-long dark age until surplus WW2 pilots' survival rafts were re-purposed by adventurers. The idea of using a packable raft for river running was reborn, but it wasn't until the 1970s when American Safety Equipment named their latest product the '**Pack Raft**' that the activity got a name. Rubber sandwiched inside canvas now became an airtight coating on ripstop nylon or just thick vinyl. Aged 55, Dick Griffiths famously trounced much of the field with such a boat in 1982's inaugural Alaska Wilderness Classic adventure race. A year later whitewater packrafting pioneer, **Roman Dial,** introduced tougher Sherpa Rafts to the Classic and wrote the first packrafting guide in 2008.

Meanwhile, behind the Iron Curtain the desire for amphibious adventures was no less strong, also using pilots' survival rafts or East German tyre-maker Pneumant's plywood-floored SB dinghies (B; Anfibio co-founder Marc Kreinacker, Hungary, 1986).

Around 2000 what became **Alpacka Rafts** responded to the dire needs of intrepid Alaskans (C; Erin McKittrick, Port Fidalgo, AK, 2004). Now made in Colorado, Alpacka remains the best-known brand, introducing many ingenious, eye-catching and widely copied innovations. Kokopelli followed in 2012 with their distinctive 8-panel hulls, as did Micro Rafting Systems (MRS) from China. Today there are well over twenty brands, mostly China-sourced from inflatable-leisure product specialists like Audac Sports. Brands now seek to outdo or undercut each other, but with all the major advances probably made, it leaves only incremental improvements and diversified model ranges to attract specialised users.

Underneath, they're all packrafts which have proved much more durable than their resemblance to short-lived pooltoys may suggest. Unlike slackrafts (p11) your TPU packraft can handle firm inflation without pinprick leaks or splits, and won't degrade into a pile of discoloured plastic in a year or two.

At it's heart a packraft remains as basic as a Bronze Age coracle, a do-it-all, carry-anywhere boat for whatever use you dare to put it to.

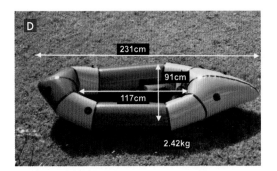

231cm

91cm

117cm

2.42kg

CONSTRUCTION & FEATURES

A packraft like the Alpacka Yak (D) is made from around ten sections, sometimes sewn then heat welded together to make the single hull chamber which is glued or welded to a thicker floor sheet. Supple **TPU** is the fabric of choice – where 'rubber meets plastic' with minimal elasticity for taut inflation, but some 'give' against sharp impacts. **PVC** is a cheaper, heavier alternative, commonly found on East European boats. It's stiffer when cold – good on the water; less good to roll up compactly. Either fabric is what makes a packraft miles better than a vinyl slackraft (p 11).

Ultralight '**crossrafts**' (L, M) are made from just three pieces of welded nylon, PU-coated on the inside, like a tent. While cheaper, the thin hull is less durable and less stiff, making them more suited to shorter crossings: more pack; less raft.

Dernier figures get bandied about to describe the fabric: '210D' for the hull, and 420 or 840D for the floor. But denier is an abstruse measure of thread weight. Many other factors come into play, not least the qualities and thickness of the coating. Easier to understand for a 210D hull is **250 gsm** (grams/metre^2; 7.3 oz/yd^2 in the US). Bigger brands commission rolls of customised TPU but keep details and sources close to their chest.

Packrafts are laboriously assembled, even if laser cutting, sewing and heat-welding rigs simplify things. This explains the high prices compared to cheaper IK or mass-produced slackrafts.

DIMENSIONS

The Yak (D) has typical packraft dimensions: a length-to-width ratio of around 2.4:1 means slow hull speeds but excellent primary stability – a big plus for first timers. And while it'll be a squeeze, a boat like this will support two small adults if needed, and will still float above water, even when full of water.

Some boats are symmetrical front to back, most have longer sterns to effectively position the paddler more centrally (and reduce whitewater back flips), while upturned bows ride over waves. An **inflatable seat base** raises you up for a good paddling posture, helped by a backrest resting against the cockpit or suspended from straps.

MAKE YOUR OWN PACKRAFT

For under £100 and a fair amount of gnashed teeth, an adept individual could make a packraft. All you need is a roll of TPU, some scissors and a **heat-sealing iron** able to reach 200°C/390°F. Along with other items, a **template** is key as the sections are fairly complex shapes.

Luckily for you, two places: diypackraft. com in Canada and iron-raft.co.uk sell **kits** for under £200. You get pre-cut pieces or marked-out sheets of selected TPU, the valve and detailed assembly videos. Above all, **practise ironing on scraps**; it's not like doing your chinos for a night out. A good weld forms a permanent molecular bond, even if gluing can plug subsequent leaks. Having eventually cobbled together a simple TiZip TPU deckbag myself (E), I'd sooner leave packraft assembly to the pros.

Some packrafts: **F** *Alpacka Yak under a smaller Alpaca. Get the right size; a snug fit matters.* **G** *Decked Anfibio Rebel 2K above a Revo self-bailing (p29) prototype; two ways to approach whitewater.* **H** *A Russian-made TPU Nortik Trekraft.* **I** *MRS 2.9m Nomad 'pakayak'; roll-up deck and fast for a packraft.* **J** *Neris decked LotaFun and BigFun EXPs with handy deck pockets.* **K** *Mekong self-bailing Jane Gin Can.* **L** *Anfibio Nano RTC crossraft (p27D) in PU nylon and a novel roll-up closure; 1002g plus seat.* **M** *Supai Canyon Flatwater; 75D PU-nylon, even lighter and under $300, but best suited to light paddlers on flatwater.*

A GOOD FIT

Like a running shoe, **a cosy fit** front-to-back and at the hips connects you with the boat for better response – something which pays off even for relaxed paddling. This way, more energy from your paddle stroke gets transferred into forward motion. Perched on a fully inflated seat base, the correct posture also sees a bend in the knee with feet braced against the front of the cockpit.

Sat upright against a door, the distance to my soles is 113cm (66") and my recent boats of between 118 and 128cm fitted me just right. Narrow front cockpits (MRS Nomad p91) have less room and hiking boots take up space, as does an inflatable backrest, sitting you further forward – no bad thing with symmetrical packrafts.

In N, a drybag was used as backrest padding to help the 150cm tall paddler get a braced fit in an Anfibio Alpha XC (120cm long cockpit). While cockpit length was fine for me too at a foot taller, being nearly twice as heavy, **buoyancy** in this symmetrical boat with compact 25cm sidetubes, was on the limit. Meanwhile, my boat at just 20cm longer overall and with the more common 28cm sidetubes was just right.

SEATBASE & BACKREST

While you can paddle a packraft sitting directly on the floor and against the back, most won't begrudge the extra **250g of a seat**, which doubles as a camp cushion, sleeping pillow – or indeed a buoyancy aid should the boat lose all air.

Sat on the floor, you sag down as in a hammock, so even taller paddlers will find the hull sides too high and wide to get a good draw from the paddle. A good posture sees your heels a little lower than you backside, so in most cases inflate the seatbase fully to get the right height.

Seatbases in black PU-coated nylon can be 'horseshoes' (O) which drain quickly so you're not sat in water, or a more complex baffled box (P) which jams in securely for better support and height. Some may still copy Alpacka's old side-laced fitting (O) but, short of dropping off waterfalls, all that's ever been needed is a simple floor buckle at the back. This enables quick removal for drying or camp use. Add a quick-release plastic Derlin clip.

Similar U-shaped **backrests** come attached to the seatbase (O); one annoyance is they flop forward as you get in so need hooking in place. A small **back pad** attached to the hull (Q) gets round this and works well against the bulk of a buoyancy vest (p24).

Counter-tensioned EVA **foam backbands** (P) are bulkier but give solid support, storage space behind and enough forward adjustment to enable short paddlers to fit snugly into longer cockpits and a central sitting position (good for trim). They also work as the front backrest on **tandem packrafts**.

Leaks aren't rare but seams can be re-sealed with an iron and small holes glued up (p30).

SLACKRAFTS

'**Slackraft**' is my invented word for the packraft which dare not speak it's name: dirt-cheap vinyl dinghies a grade above outright pooltoys, commonly sold at beach resorts for a fraction of the cost of a packraft. Squeezed out of a press in China for brands like Sevylor, Intex and Bestway, just like many packrafting pioneers, a curious beginner might look and wonder.

Not all the differences are obvious (until you paddle one). Most have **double-chamber hulls** as well as a ribbed inflatable floor – handy for safety and compliance, but 1-2 person examples (**Q**; £50) are even more over-square than the dumpiest packraft. The soft, vinyl film can handle less than 1psi but can't always fight off a blunt stick (**R**) – expect a 90-day warranty. And with one fat rounded end, the other flat like a transom, and moulded rollocks, 'dinghy' indicates a boat to be rowed. *Paddling* kayak-style sat either end, on the sides, kneeling (we tried everything) can be excruciating.

Sevylor's Trail Boat was a budget favourite and what drove Alpacka's eventual founder to produce something tougher. Meanwhile, other users cut off outer chambers to make slimmer, more compact boats (**S**), but reduced buoyancy saw this idea ill-suited to the well fed.

You can get a bit blasé with proper packrafts. On the Fitzroy (p46) I could treat my Alpacka almost like a hardshell, while Jeff had to nurse his execrable Bestway (**T**) all the way, and still had three flats. I enjoyed; he endured, but he saved hundreds and we both had a big adventure. You'll find the long version with videos on the website.

ON THE WATER: BASIC SKILLS

Packraft Day is here! Especially if alone and totally new to paddling, try out your borrowed, rented or new boat in the **safest conditions** possible. You don't want to be distracted by sketchy access, rip tides, gales or just curious onlookers with yapping dogs. Make sure your seatbase is fully inflated and remember to **top-up** once the boat has cooled on the water.

GETTING IN & OUT

The easiest way to get in is from **knee-high water** over a firm, flat underwater surface, and with a negligible current or surf. With the boat pointing left and your paddle in your left hand, lean over and place your hands either side of the cockpit, turn anticlockwise and drop onto the seat. This way you can drip-dry the feet before bringing them in. **Don't rush it**; a recipe for a comedy splash is stepping into an unsecured boat like it's a hot bath.

Getting out, as you near the shore and can see the bed coming up (probe with the paddle) lift both legs over the left side and slide out while laying the paddle across the boat with your right hand for support. You may be a bit wobbly.

FROM A JETTY OR LOW RIVERBANK

With the luxury of a **jetty**, sit alongside the boat with the paddle in your left hand or close by (**A**). Holding the near side of the boat, swing the legs in, shuffle across and, placing the right hand on the outer side, lift your weight up on your arms and legs and lower yourself in (**B**). Move gently and push yourself upwards, not outwards.

Getting out, place both palms on a jetty or claw at a grassy riverbank (**D**). Lean over the side and roll your weight onto your arms as you swing your outer leg up and over (**E**). With three limbs on land, the fourth will surely follow. You should end up in a crouch or on your knees; whatever it takes.

With strong currents or wind, clip your mooring line or leash to your PFD while ensuring it won't tangle with your legs, so you can focus on the move, knowing the packraft is secure. If you can't secure the paddle to the boat, put it ashore.

If **steep riverbanks** (**C**) can't be avoided and there's no one to help, there's no elegant way while keeping dry. Place the boat in the water and slowly roll in with paddle in hand; a packraft's stability makes this controlled tumble fairly reliable.

SITTING COMFORTABLY

Chances are you unpacked and inflated your new toy back home and have seen how you fit, sat up straight with a slight bend to the knees and feet lightly pressing forward to keep you against the backrest (F). A separate seatbase may need shuffling forward or back so you're sat right on it.

Now on the water, are the sides a bit mushy? If yes, the boat needs a top-up. With a Boston valve and a mini-pump with an extension tube (p20), that's easily done while sat in the packraft.

SETTING OFF

Holding the paddle as suggested on p23, start paddling. Almost certainly you'll notice the **bow yawing** madly left-right, a normal consequence of a flat-bottomed boat pivoting around the swinging axis of your paddle shaft (H). This subsides as you gain speed to just a few inches each way.

FLATWATER PADDLING

Until you choose to venture into technical whitewater – not for everyone but something that's initially easier to pick up in agile and stable packrafts – there really isn't much to paddling a packraft. Endeavour to place the blade *fully* in the water by your feet and draw it along the side to your hips and out, using the 'grip-release' technique explained on p23 (p23**D**).

By paddling *gently and steadily* you'll minimise front-end yawing and progress smoothly. If your boats has a **skeg** (p28) try paddling with and without to see if you can tell the difference. Then, see how you get on with 'push-paddling' technique described below; handy when battling winds or strong currents.

Until you get used to it, expect your arms to get tired, but resting is normal; it's rare to paddle non-stop for more than 20 minutes. And though it's fun, there's no need to master paddling backwards because you can easily spin a packraft around. To make a **sharp turn**, for example to swing out of the current towards the bank, apply a **stern rudder** or **draw**: either by dragging an angled blade behind you or pushing it forward in a full reverse sweep (**I**); a packraft version of a handbrake turn.

Correct your direction by either increasing the input on one side, making a light pass on the other or by trailing a blade. You'll find yourself **micro-correcting** constantly as you cruise along.

PUSH, DON'T PULL

It's intuitive to assume you **pull** a paddle through the water, like swimming. Instead, try **pushing** on the high arm so the paddle pivots at the lower hand as in **G**, pushing against a strong tide. This way you're applying leverage, rather like an oar in a rollock. You'll get the same propulsion for less strain which works better against currents.

Just don't be surprised if, in challenging whitewater (p16) you revert to yanking on the paddle with all you've got. That works too.

Falling out in such conditions, **keep hold of the paddle**. Without it you're in a car on a hill with no brakes or steering wheel. The same goes when resting on the water: leash it or stash the paddle under a bow bag (p27).

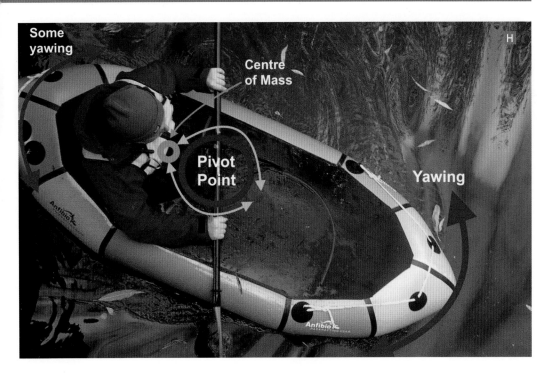

Some yawing

Centre of Mass

Pivot Point

Yawing

SLOW BOAT

If you've kayaked much you'll notice **a packraft is slow** and has zero glide. Longer boats are faster and packrafts are the shortest boats around. The complex hydrodynamics of this are best explained on YouTube, and even then you may still be baffled. A blunt, yawing bow doesn't help, so no matter how hard you paddle you won't exceed a hull speed of **3mph/5kph** (that's 2.6 knots). A sea kayak can cruise at twice that. Of course you can add river or tidal currents, and your effort will be eased or hampered by winds, but hit a patch of 'dogwater' and suddenly you can feel you're paddling a knotted bin bag.

FAST BOAT

Paddling a Kokopelli Rogue (**J**), with a friend in my Anfibio Rebel (**H**), I was a little faster. A practised paddling technique and the Rogue's long stern and tapered bow may have had an influence. Another time I was quite a lot slower than a mate in a 2.3m long MRS Nomad S1 (p12**C**). But the S1 is nearly two kilos heavier.

So yes, some **packrafts are slow** but up to a point, speed is relative. Alone you're as fast as you are, what matters is whether an exposed crossing is safe, especially at sea or on a lake where headwinds can reduce progress to just 1mph. By a shore, walking or wading may be quicker.

FASTER RIVERS, RAPIDS & WEIRS

Rivers flow fastest midway between the banks and round the outside of bends. **Rapids** occur where a riverbed steepens, drops down a step or is partially chocked, kicking up aerated waves ('white' water) and eddies. The rush of accelerating in and fighting your way out of rapids is exhilarating.

Rapids are graded from Class 1 to 6. Higher grades are usually further upstream or in a constriction like a gorge. All rapids require assessment and decisive action once committed. **Skegs** and loose leashes should be removed.

With experience, a packrafter can manage a Class 2 or an easy 3; the latter giving enough excitement without inducing a panic attack. On simple rapids a ramp of water forms a **downstream V** ending in a **wave train** that's fun to bounce over or easy to avoid. Without a deck or bailing, a Class 3 usually leaves some water in your boat.

Above Class 3 managing flat-floored packrafts takes concerted skills. Hardshells handle better here, so alongside raw nerve and technique, you need a suitable boat plus specialised gear and like-minded partners familiar with safety protocols and practised in rescues. See the book on p36.

START SMALL

First time you might try a **whitewater centre** with artificial rapids, often near urban conurbations. But in the UK at least, these places are hardshell focussed and will make you do an assessment in one (no bad thing) before letting you play.

However you do it, start on something dead easy like a Class 1 (K – quite possibly my very first packrafting rapid). At this level you're mainly looking for enough water to not run aground. The path is usually obvious; for example the channel below right – 'river left' in paddlespeak – was clearly too shallow. **Learning to read rapids** is all part of the satisfaction of honing your skills.

Again in (L), the passage of least difficulty is clear enough; less turbid flow between submerged stones which are pushing up aerated water. But just because you're getting a free ride as you're sucked in, **don't stop paddling**. If anything, **speed up** on the approach to drive the packraft through to maintain directional momentum and a light bow.

Catch a boulder and it may knock you offline. In (M) I've been flipped sideways, easily done in a spinny packraft – and of course just as easy to correct, in this case with a reverse (forward pushing) stroke (p151) with the right blade, allied with a deft hip pivot. Avoid entering any rapid **sideways** as a boat is more likely to flip as it hits impediments, but just like a 'Grand Canyon' raft, a first-timer can be forgiven for blundering through easy rapids any which way.

When a kayak rides up onto a submerged boulder, without a quick support stroke it can roll over in an instant. A packraft merely slews round and spins to a halt. Some lurching and judicious prising with a paddle (or even a leg over the side) will push you off back into the flow, where you quickly want to realign your bow downstream.

SCOUTING AHEAD

One definition of a Class 3 rapid is the need to follow a series of lines to get through, not just getting swept down an obvious downstream V. In (N) I pondered the drop from a bridge and decided my situation: alone, up a remote glen without enough protective gear – made it a bad idea, even if it may have been doable at the cost of a partly swamped boat.

GOLDILOCKS RIVERS

Like many new to paddling, I was keen to try whitewatering, but soon learnt a river has to be just right: high enough to not get stuck, but not so fast that things become unmanageable. It also helps if it's not a day's drive away.

Setting aside access and pollution issues (see p19), in the southern England such rivers are rare, with suitable conditions only in the wetter months and for just a few miles at a time. Rivers like the Dee in North Wales, or the Dart in Devon are firm favourites, but travelling for

hours to repeat a few short whitewater runs was not my thing. You can do all that just as well with an IK or a hardshell, but *only a packraft* opens up the wilds of somewhere like the Scottish Highlands.

Or, for fabulous multi-day paddles just a train ride away and interspersed with fun rapids and chutes, you can't beat the half-dozen Goldilocks rivers in southern France's Massif Central, with many more on the other side of the Rhône. More on the website.

Assessing such hazards is all part of establishing your comfort level. Raised water levels (from rain or dam releases) speed up currents which can either smother gnarly rapids or make them much more challenging as the water's force gets multiplied exponentially. **Scouting ahead on foot is a vital part of running rivers**, whatever the grade. A recce enables you to figure out a line through a complex **rock garden** (O), or spot any possible entrapment hazards like fallen trees (P).

TREES, OTHER 'STRAINERS' & EDDIES

Fast currents and inattentiveness can sweep you into fallen or **semi-submerged trees**; one of the biggest hazards to river paddlers. Known as '**strainers**' (as in 'sieves'), they less commonly include jumbled boulders or a metal grill across a sluice. Get caught against a fallen tree's branches and the current can pin you. Undecked boats reduce perceived entrapment risks, but with a foot jammed in branches, you could be dragged down by the current, unable to release yourself.

Dodging **overhanging branches** is more common, especially on the faster line around the outside of a bend. If it's too late, don't crouch forward and, above all, resist the impulse to grab a branch; you'll be pulled from your boat. If you can't avoid low boughs, slide forward, lean back and protect your face with your paddle. If you fall in **swim on your back** with **feet first** and raised up.

An **eddy** is where a current (can be tidal) spins off and back on itself. Eddy pools often form on riverbanks just below rapids (or behind big rocks O1); handy spots to 'eddy out' for a breather. You may read a lot about the perils of flipping on crossing **eddy lines** where opposing currents meet. Tippier hardshells need to adopt preferred angles and various techniques to avoid capsizing, but down at Class 2 levels, I find stable packrafts are relatively immune to crossing eddy lines.

LOCKS, CHUTES & WEIRS

Many rivers have man-made infrastructure: **locks**, often alongside **weirs** and much less often (in the UK) a **canoe chute** (Q) – a fun, portage-free way of sliding safely down a weir. Note (R's) chute entry (S) is not at all obvious.

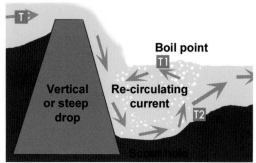

Weirs ('low-head dams' in the US) are man-made barrages, an ancient means of controlling river levels for navigation, irrigation or to generate power. A small or sloping drop (R1) can look harmless, but **high flows** can switch steeper weirs (T) into producing a lethal recirculating current called a **hydraulic jump** or 'stopper'. Heavily aerated water massively reduces buoyancy and every year swimmers and a few paddlers drown below such weirs. A churning 'boil point' (T1)

flowing upstream before being sucked down, is a danger sign, but isn't always obvious. If shooting an easy weir, **go in fast** and don't stop until you're clear. YouTube has loads of salutary videos or search: 'Safety at weirs, British Canoeing'.

Treat *all* weirs with caution and portage. Note stoppers can form in powerful natural rapids too, especially if curving downstream. If trapped, try to swim out along the river bed (T2) or work your way sideways until you can break out.

RIVER ACCESS IN ENGLAND & WALES

'There is no general Public Right of Navigation (PRN) on English and Welsh non-tidal rivers for canoeists.
Angling Trust
'Of the 42,700 miles of inland waterways in England, only 1,400 miles can be paddled uncontested.'
British Canoeing

For millennia after the invention of the wheel, waterways remained vital trade arteries as well as public rights of way or 'navigation' (PRN). Then, the industrial revolution saw a network of canals grow to transport heavy goods until railroads and eventually highways took their place.

Today, the industry of outdoor recreation benefits many more, but unlike just about any other nation (including Scotland) PRN is a thorny issue in England and Wales – and this was long before sewage pollution scandals in southern England. The feudal origins of English land ownership as well as an influential angling lobby ensure that less than 4% of rivers and canals can be paddled. Just two canals, tiny sections of four rivers as well as 150 miles of the Wye have PRN. Elsewhere, a £45 British Canoeing **Waterways licence** is required above the tide's high water point. In Scotland the 2003 Land Reform Act covered rivers and lochs; you're free to packraft responsibly almost anywhere. Learn more at riveraccessforall. co.uk. During the 1930s walkers fought similar battles to regain moorland access now taken for granted.

INFLATION, VALVES & PUMPS

Packrafts are initially inflated by screwing a big **air bag** (A) into a threaded port in the boat's hull, scooping air then scrunching the bag to fill the boat. The bag weighs next to nothing and with the knack, it takes about 8-10 scrunches and a couple of minutes. In the old days (and maybe still) you then had to unscrew the bag and quickly fit the cap before too much air escaped, then **top up** by mouth via a twist-lock elbow valve (C), as still used on seats. Once on the water all **inflatables cool and internal pressures drop a little**, requiring more topping-up or 'tempering'. It's worth it because a **firm packraft paddles much better**.

Packrafts still come with airbags, but recent years have proved that, even with the lungs of Adele belting out the new Bond theme, they can handle a little more pressure to great effect.

ONE-WAY BOSTON & RAFT VALVES

Ironically, we can thank slackrafts for the wide adoption of the **Boston valve** (B). An inexpensive and clever design that's largely reliable, they're also used in kitesurf wings and are ideally suited to the low-pressure duties in a packraft. Alpacka use their own turn-valve design.

Boston valves have a similar screw-in port for easy airbagging and quick deflation. The difference is the two-part cap (B1, 2) has an integrated soft rubber mushroom seal (B3). You can top-up by mouth (easier via a bit of garden hose G), but an actual one-way valve means a cheap balloon pump (see opposite) will eventually do a better job than your lungs.

Among others, Mekong, ROBfin (E) and Kokopelli use high-pressure 'raft valves' ('military valves' in the US), an equally proven mechanism found on better IKs, commercial rafts, RIBs and iSUP boards. Some use a bayonet fitting to secure the pump nozzle, but on a low-pressure packraft a push-fit like Leafield's popular D7 is fine. Air flow opens a poppet valve against a spring, and for deflation the valve can be locked open by pressing and turning, or with a second click (E), like a biro.

Capable of handling over 15psi (1 bar), they can seem like overkill or a bid to be different; a packraft is tight as a drum at 2psi (0.14 bar) and airbagging might take a bit more effort. But unlike a permanently fixed Boston valve base, with a tool (p31E) raft valves can be removed, making replacement or inspection easy.

ELECTRIC & MECHANICAL PUMPS

As explained, packraft inflation involves two stages: pushing in a large volume at low pressure for which an airbag is fine, followed by adding a tiny volume to attain higher pressures which airbagging won't manage though your lungs just about can.

Though airbagging is hardly arduous or prolonged, the advent of inexpensive USB rechargeable electric pumps like the 150g Flextailgear (F), mean you can set one off and do something else, inflate a sleeping mat (best not done with humid breath) and with some models, even use it as a power bank to recharge your phone. You'll easily get a dozen fills, but bring an airbag in case the pump packs up, otherwise you may pass out doing the low-pressure fill by mouth.

For the essential topping up, repurposed balloon mini-pumps have been found to work well, and enable a little over-inflation on land to eliminate the need for tempering on the water. You'll find them cheap on eBay, but not all have the long hose with a push-in adaptor that fits Boston valves. Weight can be just 120g and, if needed, the hose makes topping up on the water easy.

Larger volume boats can take a lot of topping up to get the boat taut. For that something like the burlier K-Pump Mini (G) is made for full-sized rafts and IKs, but weighs 600g and costs ten times more than a balloon pump. It'll be well suited to bigger packrafts and blows through raft valves where a balloon pump might struggle.

PADDLES

A packraft paddle's chief attribute is breaking down into **four pieces** (Anfibio Wave A) so that, like your boat, it's easily transportable on foot, by bike or on public transport.

"Strong, light, cheap: pick two" supposedly said legendary MTB pioneer, Keith Bontrager. So it is with paddles, but these days around £100 ought to cover a decent Chinese-made 4-parter to get you packing. You'll be holding the paddle up for long periods so aim for **under 1000g** (33oz), offering **durability** against the inevitable knocks and scrapes, as well as a **stiff** shaft and blade. The €125 Wave is 991g, while the two-piece Werner Corryvrecken (F1) which I prefer on day trips is just 816g but costs over £260. Once you realise packrafting won't be a passing fad, invest over £200 in a quality paddle like a Werner or something like a four-piece Aqua Bound Manta Ray (880g). Your boats may change but a good stick will last decades.

A four-piece paddle will never be as rigid as a single- or two-piece, but alloy-shaft/plastic-blade cheapies have bendy blades (B) and ever more slack joints. None of that will stop you going forward, but like an under-inflated packraft, it feels sloppy, unresponsive and wastes energy.

The stiffest, lightest material is **fibreglass**. Carbon or fibreglass shafts are warmer to hold than metal, and are ovalised or have an indexed lump on the 'control' side (see box opposite) for a good grip.

PADDLE LENGTH

You're sat low in a high-sided raft that's nearly a metre wide, so with paddle length aim on the long side, around **210-220cm** (83-87"). As a guide it's said the **height of your raised finger tips** roughly equals your ideal paddle length.

For sedate, sustained crossings – as opposed to high-energy whitewater or headwinds – **longer paddles** allow relaxed low-angles (a more horizontal paddle). But length increases leverage which can become a struggle into a headwind or against a strong current. Rather like changing down a gear on a bike, shortening the length (possible with the Wave A, among others) reduces the strain if not the effort.

All paddles come with **drip rings** at the neck of each blade, but without a deck you'll still get wet. **Waxing** the blades (C) sheds water more quickly. Give it a go, as I did, but don't be surprised if you still get wet.

BLADE OFFSET & PADDLING TECHNIQUE

Beginners often clamp the paddle shaft and jab at the water with short strokes and blades half-submerged. It works, but there's a more efficient technique. With elbows stuck out horizontally and arms bent forward at right angles, grasp the shaft equidistantly then **align the knuckles** of your 'control hand' (usually right) with the top edge of the right blade (D). The blade should curve backwards like a scoop, and if the shape is asymmetric (F), the longer corner should be uppermost.

You'll now find adjusting the opposite blade's top edge forward by about **45°** improves paddling. Most multi-section paddles have this **feathering** adjustment, be it just a second click-hole, a grooved ferrule or infinite settings (E Anfibio Wave). Some claim this helps the returning blade swing forward edge-on to reduce wind resistance. That's true; Olympic rowers do something similar, but with a two-bladed paddle it's more about **ergonomics**.

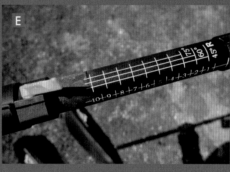

With 'zero' offset the control hand must bend awkwardly to get the best entry angle for the opposite blade. With some offset (30° for whitewater; 45° elsewhere) paddling feels more natural.

Offset blades work best with a special technique. As the controlled (right) blade dips in alongside your feet and the other raised arm begins to move forward, **loosen your left grip**. Then, when the right blade comes out by your hips, turn your right wrist up (knuckles towards you) to let the shaft slip through the left hand. Then, when the left blade enters the water, retighten your left grip and draw the fully submerged paddle back through the water to your hips. As the left blade comes out, loosen the grip again to get the right blade at the optimal entry angle. The **control hand always grips the shaft**; the other grips to draw back then loosens when swinging forward. It's a bit like shovelling sand: you dig in gripping the D-handle and the shaft, but to toss the sand off to the side you momentarily loosen the grip on the shaft and twist on the handle. Practise sat on a chair with some space around you; soon this technique becomes second nature. See also the box on p14.

Precise blade shapes are like tyre treads: for most there's not much in it. Surface areas vary ten percent either side of 650cm^2 (F2). Anything over 700cm^2 (F1) is for powering on in fast-moving water, though I find works for day paddles too.

In the end what counts are **taut joints, stiff shafts** and blades, **feathering** as well as durability – all without weighing a ton. The two chipped and scratched paddles (right) have a combined age of over 25 years and have as long left in them.

BUOYANCY VESTS

Commonly called 'lifejackets' but more neutrally known as **buoyancy vests** or personal floatation devices (PFDs), in this book you'll find the odd image of packrafters not wearing them. In some places wearing PFDs on the water is the law. In the UK there are no such regulations but even though you'll see stand-up paddle boarders and rowers in all sorts of craft not wearing them, get in the habit of **always wearing a PFD**.

Nervous beginners in tippy hardshells don't need much persuasion because, once capsized these boats are very difficult to drain and remount from deep water without help. By comparison a packraft is exceedingly stable on flat water and easy to flip back upright and re-enter without help, either by dipping down and launching upwards and over with your arms, kicking with all you've got, or doing the same coming from the side.

If nothing else, the half-millimetre of TPU that keeps your single-chamber boat afloat ought to concentrate the mind because falling out of any boat, **cold water shock** can temporarily paralyse your breathing and drown you in minutes, while your 3-kilo packraft gets whisked away by the wind. The buoyancy a PFD provides in these traumatic moments of panicked gasping helps keep your head up so you don't swallow water. Read rnli.org/safety/know-the-risks/cold-water-shock and remember, a deep river or lake may well be colder than the sea.

GET A PFD YOU WILL WEAR

One reason PFDs are dutifully bought but not always worn is that the cheapest ones feel like wearing a polystyrene waistcoat. So spend from £80 upwards on a cushy PFD that's the **right size** and **rating** (I) for you and your weight, looks and **feels good** to wear, **adjusts** easily in various axes, and has at least one **pocket** (G, H).

Safety benefits aside, **bright colours** look better in photos, front zips are more versatile than pull-overs, while front clips keep a vest closed even with the zip open – handy when it's warm.

Inflatable vests like Anfibio's 450g twin-chamber Buoy Boy (H) don't claim to be certified, but on *flatwater* are unobtrusive, pack small and have handy stash nets, plus a crotch strap to stop it riding up. Astral's foam V-Eight has a similar high-back design suited to packraft backrests.

CLOTHING ON THE WATER

As well as paddling the rivers, lochs and coasts, packrafting can involve clambering over hill and dale which can mean a lot of clobber to cart around on your back. There's more about trekking and camping gear on p32; here's the rest of what you need while paddling.

'Dress for the water not the air [temperature]' goes the paddling adage. But just as with wearing PFDs, wisely or not, some evaluate the likelihood and consequences of falling in by the weather on the day. On a balmy summer's paddle in southern Europe you'll be dressing against sunburn not cold-water shock, and will relish a cooling dip. Meanwhile, in the wilds of Scandinavia or similar latitudes, a drysuit is a good idea at any time of year.

Your PFD keeps you warm (too warm at times; another reason they get ditched), but dress in **synthetic fabrics** which dry quickly and, unlike cotton, won't draw away body heat when soaked.

WATERPROOFS

Here the minimal extra weight of a deck pays off in keeping your legs dry, if you want them so. Combine that with your **hiking jacket** (J) and your outfit is simplified for non-whitewater use. But at some point you're going to be getting in and out, which can include tottering on wet boulders or steep banks (p12B) in a doomed bid to keep the feet dry – and end up falling in anyway.

Wading in is less risky so either roll up the trousers, wear shorts and wet shoes, or use kayaking over-trousers. Then wrap up as exposed legs and wet feet don't generate much heat.

Wet suits and thinner neoprene tops get clammy so are best suited to thrashing about in whitewater. High-waisted, breathable 'dry pants' (L) are less clingy, but consider **integrated 'socks'** over ankle seals, so you're sealed from toe to waist. Most come with socks taped up from sections of membrane fabric, but who needs breathable feet sat in a boat? You want bomb-proof impermeability, so choose **latex** (K, L); which is easily repaired with a dab of sealant. Latex benefits from **anti-UV spray** once in a while, but note that neither sock types are suited for prolonged walks.

DRYSUIT

A full-weight whitewater drysuit is a reassuring cocoon but is bulky and needs internal braces to hold it up. Something like Anfibio's one-kilo PackSuit (K) is less likely to be left behind to save weight on a chilly, multi-day trip. Better a less insulating thin drysuit than none at all. Wrists are latex; the neck is neoprene which may seep but is less choking to wear all day. In a fleece onesie and a merino top, a mid-winter paddle (p15J) is cosy without feeling trussed up like a lamb joint. Just don't assume you can bob around indefinitely.

Be gentle with stiff brass or plastic **zips** (lube with wax or silicon grease) and male or female, as your own 'seals' weaken with the advancing years, you won't regret having a **relief zip** (K).

FOOTWEAR

Old trainers or zip-up neoprene booties work, but once flooded, wellies (M1) can drag you down. Enclosed sandals (Teva Omniums M2) or even Crocs **drain** quickly. If needed, let the socks do the warming: SealSkinz-type membrane socks have limited life spans but, like wool, retain heat once soaked. For all-terrain walking footwear see p35.

OUTFITTING & LOAD CARRYING

All packrafts should have half-a-dozen **attachment loops (A)** fixed to the hull and maybe more inside. The four at the bow are most useful to secure a big pack (as on the front cover) where it balances a boat out nicely. Some owners also thread **grab lines (A)** through the front and rear tabs; it certainly makes the boat easier for two to carry.

CARRYING FULL LOADS

Loading up, always consider **what would happen if the boat flips** – especially in strong currents or high winds. Secure everything that matters to the boat; a side benefit is bags (and leashed paddles) will slow down a packraft that might otherwise blow away faster than you can swim.

Capsized, you may need to remove a bow bag fast, perhaps for flotation if the boat loses all air. Alpacka offered the Packtach system; originally a quick-release buckle (**B**, p34**G**), now simple cleats to quickly unhitch a bag. It's handy for portages or at the end of a long, cold day, too.

SUBMERSIBLE BAGGAGE

Alone on open water, an exterior bag that's as airtight as your boat offers reassuring **emergency buoyancy**. No matter how tightly rolled, a regular 'dry' bag leaks when squeezed. Look into TiZip bags from Ortlieb or Watershed's press-and-seal 'ZipDry' closures (an oversized version of a ZipLoc freezer bag). They are bomb-proof.

IN-HULL STORAGE

Another radical and again, widely copied Alpacka innovation was storing gear **inside the voluminous hull**, accessed via a waterproof TiZip or similar in the boat's stern (**C**). Called the Cargo Fly, clever though the idea was, I was never won over by the idea of fitting a zip into a lightly pressurised, single-chamber raft which gets packed and unpacked on sandy shores and riverbanks. Following warranty claims, there's now a detailed page on the intricacies of Cargo Fly care and maintenance. It's not just a matter of cleaning grit stuck to over-lubed teeth, but a fungus that can degrade the closure if left damp for too long. Not all manufacturers offering a hull zip option include them in their warranties.

Over the years zips or care guidance have

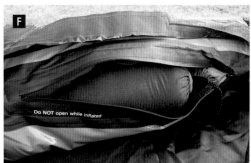

improved because the benefits are clear: space for three times more gear than you could carry, with everything secure and dry. Without a bag over the bow, **visibility** is improved; important when threading through rapids or dodging other obstacles. The boat is also more streamlined into the wind and the **centre of gravity is lowered**, greatly benefiting stability in rough water or when sailing (p40). A loaded boat can also seem empty, handy when left unattended with others around.

You don't just sling stuff in like the boot of a car; it'll roll around or may bunch up on one side. Use the long storage bags which should be included and, when full, clip them to a fitting inside the hull. If you have a hull-zip installed after purchase (easily done), make sure such a tab is fitted (like the zip, it will probably need gluing as, these days, most TPU packrafts don't have a heat-weldable coating on the inside). A novel, zip-free way of achieving the same result is a roll-top packraft, like Anfibio's Nano RTC crossraft (**D**).

Drawbacks include a heavy boat when packed which makes arduous or long portages (**E**) more awkward unless you unload. Plus every time you access the gear in the hull (typically overnight) you'll have to re-inflate the boat. All the more

reason to carry a mini electric pump (p21 **F**).

Nortik and Anfibio came up with what I consider a better idea: a pair of huge, **airtight zip pockets** fitted into the side tubes (**F**). Anfibio's IPX7-rated zips may be less airtight than a hull MasterSeal TiZip, but are out of the dirt and separated from the hull chamber by the airtight pocket. On my Anfibio 2K, the 70-litre TubeBags easily swallow multi-day camping loads. And as you inflate a packed boat with zips just ajar, the pocket's contents are pressure-sealed into place; no need for securing straps. Once inflated, don't forget to zip right up.

DAY ACCESS STORAGE

In the hull and out of the way is handy, and not just on a multi-day trip, but you'll still need to stash or access stuff on the water. There's only so much you can cram in you PFD's pockets or under your knees, but these days many packraft outfitters make **bow bags** which are easily fitted with re-usable zip-ties to a packraft's front loops. Anfibio's DeckPack (**G**) has an IPX7-rated zip accessing about 20 litres of storage – enough for your day needs including lunch and cooking gear. Add a sling and it converts into an as-useful **shoulder bag** on the trail or when away from the boat.

DO YOU NEED A DECK?

It's an inflatable so worries of the boat filling up then sinking are unfounded but yes, **you will get wet** from paddle drips and splashes. Although you may rarely use it, a **removable/roll-back deck** allows you to grow with your abilities and tackle more challenging waters or any weather – or just feel cosy on chillier flatwater paddles. They're the **best of both worlds**, but because a packraft can't be easily rolled back up when capsized (unlike slimmer hardshells with spray decks), **practise getting out quickly** and smoothly before the day comes when you might want to do so in a hurry.

Preferring the simplicity of open boats, it took me a while to get used to decks. Setting aside the hemmed-in feeling, the thin fabric and skinny zippers can feel flimsy and easy to snag. On a cold day, I'd sooner wear a drysuit (p15J).

Alpacka's first decks could be easily rolled up (**H**) and deployed on the water, or zipped right off (p10**P**). Since called '**Cruiser decks**' (**I**) and widely copied, a zip runs in a 'J' from the front right, back and behind you to alongside your left hip. From here the deck's left edge is held down with velcro and has a **grab loop** to pull it open quickly and

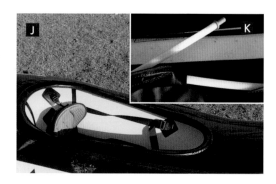

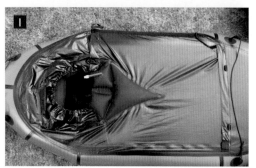

easily. A zip or velcro attaches the front edge to the fixed flap over the bow, and more velcro carries on up the side of a **torso tube** which stays up with elastic or a cinch cord (there must be no braces). An inflatable triangular 'codpiece' (**I**) helps shed water that pools on the flat deck.

Cruiser decks are a well thought-out design and, with care, will last longer than you'd expect, but won't keep you bone dry in rough water or heavy rain, just delay getting a bit damp.

Meanwhile, a **whitewater deck** (**J**) seeks to imitate hardshell kayaks with an oval hatch in a deck that's either permanently fitted (the hardcore option) or zips off and may be entirely removable (**J**). On p9 **G** shows both versions.

The hatch's rim or **coaming** has a sleeve into which you slide and close up a bendy coaming hoop, best made from pre-curved sections of nylon (**K**) and/or glass-fibre tubing. The rod provides a firm raised lip over which you can hook an elasticated kayaking **spray skirt** of matching diameter. These skirts seal best to a kayaking top or drysuit with a smooth waistband. At the front all spray skirts have a **grab loop** to yank back when you need to eject (or just get out). You'll need just the right tension for the skirt to stay in place as you do your moves, but not so tight you can't ease it on without help, or pull off with minimal effort.

SKEG (TRACKING FIN)

As shown on p15**H**, packrafts pivot as you paddle but **track** (go where they're pointed) well enough, so unlike on an IK, the benefits of a slip-on **skeg** (**N**) are less obvious. But on longer boats as well as for open crossings and sailing (p40) a skeg may well help keep the boat on line.

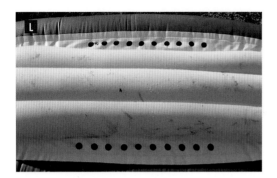

SELF-BAILING FLOORS

If you're especially into whitewater, another way to deal with the boat getting swamped is a **self-bailing floor**, as found on commercial whitewater rafts and hardshell sit-on-top kayaks.

Holes along the floor's edge combined with a raised, inflated floor – as on the ROBfin (**L**) – or a separate inflated pad (**M**) sit you above the water while also displacing that water. What pours in drains out nearly as fast. You'll soon be soaked of course, but that's what drysuits or warm summer days are for. Best of all, there's no deck to pull back. Particularly with the smaller kayak-type hatches, that can be a big plus.

Anfibio's distinctive twin-tailed Revo (p9G) bails via a big **funnel** under the seat (**N**), an idea used on some inflatable canoes. The principle is the same as multiple holes: a floor pad raises the paddler as well as reduces the volume of carried water so you're not hauling its extra weight.

Usefully, the funnel can be pulled into the boat, rolled up and clipped shut like a drybag closure, so making a regular 'displacement boat' with the smoother floor producing less drag in the water, a factor with other self-bailing methods.

THIGH STRAPS

While a snug fit in your packraft helps with the agility needed to navigate easier rapids, as things get more lively you'll miss the solid connection and control from knees braced under the deck of a hardshell kayak. A thin deck isn't the same thing, but taut **thigh straps** (**M**) attached to the hull sides can enable the hip-flicking bracing needed to stabilise or steer a packraft, and even pull it up from a capsize. Straps aid good propulsion too; get used to them and you may find your packraft too 'loose' without them. **Entrapment** is a risk; have a rescue knife (p37) attached to your PFD.

OTHER IDEAS

A **mooring line** is also handy for wading, towing or as a paddle leash on open water. Remove or ziptie it up in whitewater. Heavier paddlers may wear the floor when scraping through shallows. An added exterior **buttpatch** or just some tape (p30) will preserve the floor's coating. Similarly, a foam **heel pad** (**O**) stops hard heels causing pinch-impacts on submerged edges. And while it's better to have the right-sized boat, shorter paddlers may like to fit an **inflatable foot brace** (**P**).

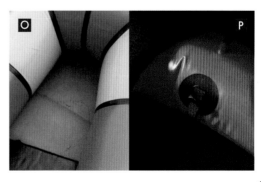

PACKRAFT CARE & REPAIR

There can't be many forms of transport as basic as a packraft: an elliptical airtight ring fitted with a plug, stuck to a floor to stop you falling through. On top of ease of storage, transportation and use, this simplicity also brings benefits in minimal maintenance and straightforward repairs.

RINSE & DRY

Look after your packraft as you would your other outdoor gear: after a paddle, rinse in freshwater and **dry fully** before long-term storage. Doing so rinses out grit which may find it's way into valve caps or under lifting seams (particularly if glued, not heat-welded) and flushes out organic matter (A) that will rot, producing odours and possible stains (though unlikely to compromise the integrity of your boat). The only particle-trapping place in a packraft is inside at **the floor-hull join** where the two surfaces may be pressed together. Especially if coming off a sandy beach, get right in there to flush out any grains.

You don't need to do all this when rolling up after one paddle before trekking off to the next, but within a day or two of the trip's end. Heading home, at least **rinse the boat** (or leave it out in the rain). Shiny TPU dries quickly in the warm sun and a breeze (B) and after suspending a boat, a **microfibre cloth** soaks up most of what pools at the lowest point, leaving just a final airing before rolling up loosely for next time.

LEAKS

A leak will either be a failure in the boat's seams – possibly a warranty claim – or a puncture in the hull or floor that's part of the game. Inflation valves can also play up; it's usually grit on the seal.

The advent of topping-up pumps can produce a nice, taut boat but will expose weak or poorly sealed seams, especially flat seams in PU nylon crossrafts and all seats (F). It's something to think about before inflating your packraft as hard as a basketball when it's 33°C in the shade.

The quickest fix to the hull is applying **tape** to a clean, dry surface; it can even be a considered a permanent repair. DuPont's **Tyvek** is an established favourite, but the 25m rolls are costly in the UK and more than you'll ever need unless you're fixing up the roof. Gorilla Waterproof Patch & Seal Tape comes in wider 3-metre rolls and will work below the waterline. Half-a-metre stashed dry in your kit will do. I just found two Tenacious Tape patches and **alcohol swabs** (C) in my packraft bag which have been there so long I'd forgotten what they were. Taped **floor repairs** are best done inside the boat. Round off pointed corners to avoid peeling.

In fact any smooth surfaced and super sticky vinyl tape will get you home, especially on a pinprick hole. Gorilla Tape fixed an abrasion leak in the vulnerable stern of a PU-nylon crossraft (D), but like lesser duct tapes, it will shrivel and dry over time.

Anything in or near a taped seam will need a couple of inches of overlap, as will short tears. Should your boat get swiped by a bear claw one night (as happened to Erin M in the Aleutians; p7C), you'll need to stitch up the big gash or 'L' tear with **needle and thread**. Taping the uncoated inside, followed by the exterior can also work.

VALVES & CAPS

Made redundant by Boston or raft valves (in the hull at least), **stem valves** – either twist-lock or one-way (p21C, D) are nowadays only used in seats. Early Alpacka hull twist-locks were mushy and easily overtightened. Current Kokopelli seat stems feel much sturdier. If they play up, cut off the old one and glue in a new valve head. Or just fold the valve neck over and cinch down with a zip-tie.

Loose **valve caps** were also easily lost – again solved by a Boston's integrated lanyard. As with in-hull storage zips, it pays to keep any main valve assembly away from loose debris. If this happens, brush and rinse thoroughly as the rubber seals in the caps can trap sand grains. Inspect and clean or replace. All raft valves need special removal tools (E Leafield) for full inspection.

GLUED & HEAT-WELDED REPAIRS

Sometimes tape won't work or won't last, so use a urethane sealant/adhesive like Stormsure or **Aquasure** (C; 'Aquaseal' in North America) from gearaid.eu, the same people behind Tenacious Tape. Follow the instructions carefully as this stuff takes hours to cure; I've even used it to stick PVC (plastic) to hypalon (rubber), but in most cases you'll be applying a blob on a pinprick hole or gluing down a lifting seam or tape which can't be heat sealed as the coating is exposed and will melt (only apply hot irons to uncoated surfaces).

Unless you can get inside the boat via a removed valve hole or a hull zip, the only things that can be **heat sealed** using a clothes iron (or a spoon heated over a camping stove) are separated seams on seats (F), or PU-nylon crossraft hulls (D) (also p9L, M).

A packraft lashed outside a backpack is far more likely to suffer damage, by **snagging** or **abrasion** (particularly tightly folded PVC) than when on the water. This applies in transit as well as when clambering over deer fences. Stuffing your vulnerable deflated boat inside a thick PVC drybag means one less thing to worry about.

ON THE TRAIL: BASIC GEAR

If you've no intention of ever walking far and wild camping, or you're an experienced mountain walker (as many new to packrafting are) you can skip this bit. And while I'm a veteran to all this, you will find my choices highly subjective.

KEEPING IT LIGHT

A packrafting payload adds up to some **5kg** (11 lbs); a crossraft under 3kg. That's a lot on top of a multi-day backpacking load of around 10-12kg (26.5 lbs). At least you'll never be far from annoyingly heavy water. Start doing much of this over tough terrain and very soon you'll alight upon the Golden Truth of Packrafting: **paddle when you can; walk when you must.**

SHELTER: TENT, BAG, MAT

If it was only the need to shelter from gently falling rain, a silnylon **tarp** or even your packraft supported by your paddle and some Dyneema cord might suffice. Sadly, in the temperate latitudes so well suited to packraft exploring, there will be wind to chill you and bugs to torment you. Some manage with a **bivi bag**, but when you add being weather-bound on a remote beach, the benefits of an actual **tent** (and a book) are well proven, especially now modern design and materials have reduced tent weights and bulk to staggeringly low levels. There are scores of tents to chose from; here are some things to consider:
- All-in-one pitching
- <2kg per person, and side entry
- The length and height to stretch out and sit up
- Ability to pitch inner or outer only
- Easily-packable short tent pole sections

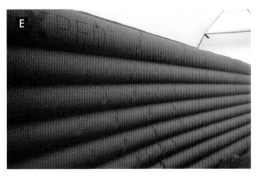

You can add using a groundsheet protecting **footprint** (floor sheet) and **self-standing** to enable pitching on hard surfaces, but normally the fly will need at least two pegs. I suspect that, like 'sweat-free' backpacks, **condensation**-reducing vents are dubiously effective: some mornings a fly is drenched with everything open; the next it's bone dry (probably due to a breeze). The same goes for loads of **porch space**. An upturned packraft is a handy shed for extra clobber and anyway, wet items under the fly just add condensation.

Having had loads of tents – including exotic single-skinners that both breathed like a bell jar and leaked like a sieve – I learnt a *packrafting* shelter really must be compact and light, even at a cost to comfort. That'll be £400+, please. For the moment Terra Nova's Laser Compact (**A3, B**) fulfils most of my criteria. The 'two-person' claim is ludicrous, but at 1.25kg and the size of a rugby ball, once I'd hand-sealed the main seam and replaced the pegs with MSR Groundhogs, all-weather camping was tolerable.

More spacious all round and fit for two at a pinch, is MSR's ever-popular Hubba Hubba which, like the best tents, can be pitched inner

only (**C**) in an arid area, or outer only to save some weight and bulk (providing the bug torment index is low). Just make sure the fly's hydrostatic head (impermeability) rating is around 3000mm or more, otherwise like the old Vaude (**D**), it may need a bit of help during summer downpours. That Vaude is a **three-pole design** which adds **stability** during strong winds by reducing large, unsupported flanks. On windy nights the flapping of my previous Hilleberg Nallo was maddening. Bring **earplugs**.

For sleeping, I still believe you can't beat goose down for warmth, comfort and compression, despite the risks of it getting soaked. A 1-kilo **down bag** (**A1**) is barely bigger than the Laser (**A3**). If you're cold, wear a hat or more clothes.

Yes, people have tried using a packraft as a sleeping mat and even a shelter, but most find it doesn't work in the long run. These days I don't begrudge the one-kilo of something like a full length Exped Synmat XP 9LW **sleeping mat** (**A2, E**) once you factor in the eight hours spent lying on it. Though bulky, a 9cm mat like this effectively increases your sleeping bag's rating by minimising heat lost through the cold ground.

BACKPACK

If you already own a large backpack, give it a go for packrafting overnighters. That's what I originally did and what my occasional travel chums still do, lashing stuff on the outside (**F**) as needed. The thing is, everything inside wants to be sealed not just for rain (with oversized 'shower caps') but possible, if brief, **submersion**. As mentioned, even if it may never happen, anticipating this sets the mind at rest, just like wearing a PFD.

I started with a giant drybag (**G**), going further down the 'bags-within-bags' rabbit hole before discovering Watershed's 90-litre Ultimate Ditch Bag (p4). With it's survival-suit zip, you could tow that bag like a tender. Paddling lonesome lochs, the UDB's rock-solid submersability gave back-up buoyancy, but on the trail the basic, unstable harness was hard on the shoulders.

Full-sized packs work by using a **stiff frame or plate** linking hip belt to shoulder straps to take the weight **low on your hips**, not hanging from your shoulders. Combined with a chest strap, the load is pulled close to your back *but shoulders take little weight*. Once external alloy packframes did this job not very comfortably, since then discreet

stiffening elements have been cleverly engineered into pack's anatomically-contoured bodies. With lashings of supposedly sweat-reducing, mesh-backed padding, correctly sized and adjusted, articulated hip belts move with your spine to make all-terrain load-hauling as comfortable as can be, but they're still made for backpackers, not amphibious packrafters.

PACK HARNESS

An idea popular in North America is a **pack harness**: a backpack without the pack, just the stiffened frame with the padded straps (**H**). To that you can lash a big dry bag (**I**), an IK, a moose head or whatever you like. Anfibio in Germany sells a couple of US-branded pack harnesses.

Carrying a Sea to Summit 65-litre TPU drybag and an Anfibio packraft, the Flex PR from Six Moons (**H, I**) is one of the few harnesses designed for packrafting. With no less than nine pockets, including a sleeve for your four-part paddle, it'll slip past the zip of most in-hull storage systems better than a regular backpack, and has the all-important straps at the base to attach your boat.

FOOTWEAR

Traversing rough terrain with a packrafting load stresses already hard-pressed feet. Add the desire to keep them dry across bogs or when getting on and off the water complicates matters further. Crossing a sodden watershed in 'self-bailing' shoes (p25**M2**) soon exceeds their limits. Smooth soles slip, as will lightweight closures until bogs suck the shoe right off your foot.

Last time I looked it's virtually impossible to buy non-leather mountain-hiking boots without a magical membrane that's rendered useless by stepping in just six inches of water. Once soaked, a membrane boot takes ages to dry.

Having experimented over the years, I've settled on membrane-free **desert boots** from Meindl or Lowa (**J**) which combine a stiff rugged sole for grip, rocky terrain and proper support. If needed, Seal Skinz membrane socks work, while they last.

Membrane or not, the most important thing is a boot that fits you well for days at a time. Most come with flimsy insoles; though expensive, after-market **heat-mouldable insoles** form to your unique podiatric anatomy and can transform any boot into all-day slippers.

COOKING

For simplicity you can't beat the ubiquitous **butane canisters** with compact, folding, screw-on burners and a thick **foil windshield** to maximise efficiency. Some burners come with built-in piezo igniters (**L1**), but carry a **back-up lighter** or two. It can be hard to gauge consumption so **two smaller cans** are better than one big one. These aren't allowed in airplane holds (or even Eurostar) which means sourcing gas at the other end. And in rural France the popular Campingaz cans are incompatible, so factor in a Campingaz burner too.

Solid fuel ethanol fire-starters like FireDragon (**L2**) are costlier than gas, but both faster and less toxic than hexamine tablets. Pressed into an *airtight*, screw-top tin (**L3**) you get an easy-lighting, pocket 'day-stove' (**M**) to save the canister gas. See the website for more on stoves.

With **food**, preferences are widespread but a good start is home-made granola loaded with nuts and fruit and milk powder, plus **dehydrated main meals** (**L4**). Aim for unapologetically **high calories** and experiment to find what gets you drooling because, after a few too many days of 'bag food', even roadkill starts looking appetising.

SAFETY & WEATHER

So far packrafts have escaped the 'pooltoy deathtrap' stigma, probably due to their rarity, expense and the type of person attracted to the activity. Few will spend hundreds to goof about drunk off a crowded beach on a windy day.

PACKRAFT LIMITATIONS

The dangers of packrafting are common to all paddlers: losing control of, or contact with, your boat due to strong currents, unmanageable hazards or fierce winds and waves, then not having the gear, skills or support to save yourself. For years (and maybe still) Alpacka's cautious advice was never paddle out further than you could swim back, but time has shown that fears of sudden **catastrophic deflation** are unfounded.

On **fast-moving rivers**, currents combined with previously mentioned perils like weirs, fallen trees and thundering rapids have seen fatalities. In this setting, **entrapment** has proved a particular risk. On **open water** it's waves caused by strong winds or tidal races that result in capsize and **separation**; the opposite of entrapment.

IS IT SAFE?

You might now wonder: is it even possible to enjoy packrafting without taking risks? In my experience, absolutely. The key is **recognising your limitations** – especially if **alone** – and **knowing when to revise the plan**, something I learnt aged 21 in

the middle of the Sahara. Decades later, from my very first packrafting overnighter to my most recent, I've been happy to turn back or tramp on for miles when I wasn't fully confident of dealing with conditions on the water, or where they might lead me. So far I've not had a 'moment' in a packraft, while having enjoyed some of my most memorable adventures around the world. If you think your own interests are more focused towards whitewater, track down Luc Mehl's comprehensive 450-page *Packraft Handbook*, or visit thingstolucat.com.

As a total beginner to paddling, signing up for an **instructional packrafting course** (A) is also well worth the expense. Such courses are cropping up in places where packrafting is becoming popular. The lessons you'll learn from seasoned pros should stay with you for good.

SAFETY GEAR

While dependant on your plans and attitude, here's a checklist to tick off (excluding hard whitewater). It's especially applicable if going alone or to a place you've not been to before.

- PFD with rescue items (B)
- *Accessible* phone in a waterproof case (B1), switched off or with a means to recharge
- Weather forecast (and tide times)
- Watch, GPS/satellite messenger, compass
- Submersible bag or case
- Appropriate clothing for the day and route
- Inflation pump and repair kit
- Mooring line/leash (calm or open water)
- Bailing jug or big cup (undecked; open water)
- Map, river guide or route plan (see p45)
- Accessible snacks and drinking water (at sea)

The most important of these are your PFD, an *accessible* phone (B1) and a weather forecast if heading for open water. Your PFD should have a **rescue knife** (B2; or less 'knifey' hook knife B3, sheath not shown) plus a referee **whistle** (B4, Acme or Fox) that puts out a piercing blast few can ignore. Knives risk confiscation, but in context the blunt-nosed, green NRS Pilot Knife (B2) poses little risk to your boat. On a long open water crossing you may want to fit a **skeg**.

KEEPING IN TOUCH

Though it depends on the type of trip, for most packrafters the risk of **drowning** is far greater than the need for rescue. Down in the deeper lochs of northwest Scotland you can go days without a mobile signal, by which time the granular accuracy of a possibly vital weather forecasts is lost. Sea paddlers use VHF radios which in the UK can receive Coastguard weather bulletins every three hours with line-of-sight to a mast. By far the most reliable device, short of a satellite phone, is a **two-way satellite messenger** (C) like a Garmin inReach Mini (C1) used with a phone's keyboard. This way, someone back home can text weather updates at agreed times, while also being a much better person to respond to your emergency than you pressing the built-in panic button and waiting.

WEATHER

On a river the weather's not so critical: it's either a nice day (a high pressure system) or it isn't. But especially on open water, learning to interpret weather patterns is important. One thing I've found: don't rely on just one forecast; it may be handy for laundry days, but not for paddling.

THE WIND

On open water, be it big lakes, remote lochs or the coast, the direction and strength of the wind dictate whether it's wise to get on the water. In my experience anything above **10mph** (Force 3; a 'gentle breeze' on the Beaufort Scale) requires some commitment and if it's **blowing offshore**, stay on land. Ten mph doesn't sound much, but **gusts** are typically half as strong again. In the UK the perennial southwesterly from the Atlantic blows fairly steadily. A drier **easterly** from the continent can be more irregular and gusty.

By the time a headwind hits 20mph (Force 4) you're moving at 1mph and will wonder how long you can sustain this. Wind speed can be hard to judge without experience, but **metres per second** are more easily visualised, and doubled plus 10% equal miles per hour. Lake or sea, once **whitecaps** start forming on wave crests it may be time to revise the plan. Any steep-sided loch or fjord can funnel waves over a metre high at which point things get very sketchy. If caught out, 'raft up': hold on to each other's boats for stability.

Battling a 'safe' headwind, it can be satisfying to knuckle down and inch towards your goal, though at times cresting a wave into a gust feels like a packraft could be flipped over backwards. Strong **sidewinds** are harder to manage, as waves break over the sides and the boat pitches left and right. Better to point into the wind and ferry sideways.

Strong **backwinds** can be frustrating too once they start push the stern round as it lifts over wave crests. Bulky sterns slew sideways, requiring constant and exhausting correction. Now could be time to head for shore or unfurl your downwind sail (p40).

BIKERAFTING

by Rob Estivill

Early on, a packraft's **stability** and **portability** gave birth to the idea of transporting a bicycle on the boat and vice versa. The advantages of this symbiotic relationship are many, but boil down to potentially faster mobility and an increased range on land, at a minimal cost on calmer waters (A). These facts open up itineraries long or short which wouldn't be possible on foot alone.

For those from a paddling background, it's a fun way for getting between take-out and put-in, solving the age-old problem of **shuttling** back to the start point when other transport options are scarce. For the cyclist, packrafting adds a thrilling way to discover new adventures, enabling water crossings or transits when there was no alternative. And as a means of **exercise**, paddling and pedalling are complementary activities, working both upper and lower body muscles on the same trip. **Bikerafting** gives you the freedom to plot your entire itinerary at your own pace.

One of the biggest hurdles for beginners is overcoming the perceived complications of choosing and organising two sets of gear. Trade-offs are necessary, due to the lack of specifically designed products. The best way to learn is to give it a go on short, simple trips, but here are some tips to make things easier.

A bike on a packraft increases the danger of snagging on branches or other river hazards. The added weight and higher centre of gravity means it's also much harder to right a capsized boat (if otherwise unloaded, probably best done by flipping the stern up over the semi-submerged bow). That's not something you want to do too often so choose lakes (C) and shorelines away from strong winds, or rivers up to Class 2 (A, E).

Your bike will get wet, so check there are no electronics on the frame. If there are, remove and put them in a dry bag with your other valuables before pushing off. **Lubricate** all moving parts more frequently and drain and dry the bike after each water-bound adventure, especially after a saltwater paddle where an all-out freshwater rinse or dip would be worthwhile.

Choosing a boat, an open-decked model with a broad bow is a good starting point, but this covers nearly all packrafts. If travelling, in-hull storage or a **longer packraft** will keep loads low.

STRAPPING ON

To attach the bike, depending on the type – folding, gravel, MTB – remove one or both wheels if necessary and position one of the pedals in the boat with the chainwheel uppermost, then rest the frame on the sides. The wheels can then be piled on top and everything lashed down (B). Obviously be careful nothing sharp is pressing on the hull and that the load **won't shift in rough water**.

Back on land, attaching the packraft to your bike, it can go at the front (best with flat-bar MTBs), in a saddle bag (gravel or roadbikes) or on a rear rack (D). Again, be careful the boat is

secured and isolated from any possible abrasion or sharp points. Or for short, easy rides just use a backpack. These steps can be daunting for beginners, so expect some experimentation to find your optimal set-up on land and water, then stick with it. **Don't rush loading** and **take extra straps**.

On all but the roughest terrain, pedalling will be faster than paddling, but it can also use much more energy, and cross-country, be more arduous than walking, so plan accordingly.

In terms of distance, ride a longer loop on the bike and paddle a nice section in the raft, giving yourself enough time to convert from land to water. Once you've got the basics down, the possibilities of bikerafting, from full work-out day trips (E) to extended travels, are endless!

PACKRAFT SAILING

WE ARE SAILING

It won't take hours of sluggish paddling before you ponder harnessing a tail wind to move things along (**A**). A breezy lake is a good place to safely try **downwind sailing**. Things happen fast, so be sure your **paddle** is firmly in hand, leashed or otherwise stashed.

WindPaddle (**C1**, **E**) was the original flip-out disc sail before knock-offs flooded in. It works like those pop-up tents: a folded hoop springs open into a huge dished sail. The key is the springy composite batten which can withstand three wince-inducing twists but unfurled, supports a taut sail. Today, among others, Anfibio in Germany produce the similar **PackSail**. Cheapies use thin, GRP rods that wobble about and soon snap.

A 1.2m WindPaddle 2 weighs under **400g** and is around 41cm (16") folded. That's still a fairly awkward shape to stash, so Anfibio also came up with the packraft-friendly **AirSail** (**B**, **C2**, **D**) supported by an inflatable ring that makes it much easier to pack, and inflates with your top-up mini-pump (p21**F**). But on a normal sized packraft (unlike **D**), it can be awkward to stow on the water – and there'll be times when you want to do that in a hurry, or redeploy as quickly. Having tried both, I'd sooner get a twist-and-fold batten sail.

A packraft may be light but it glides like a piano, so don't be cautious: get a big sail of at least 1.2 metres; you'll need that surface area to haul your boat along. To gain more height where there's more wind, I used to rig my WindPaddle loose on the front-most loops, but found stronger gusts would set it fluttering madly from side to side. Attaching the sail tautly to the bow (**B**) largely eliminated that.

ARE WE SAILING?

The problem with wind is that it rarely blows steadily for long, and these sails have narrow wind-speed windows (as well as handy windows, too). A gust might whoosh you along for a few thrilling moments, then drop to nothing. Along with steering away from other boats or the shore, micro-managing this can take constant attention.

A sail draped over your knees gets in the way of paddling so folding it away wants to be easily done; one of the drawbacks of the AirSail. To fully fold a batten sail three times then loop on the retaining sling and not lose your paddle while being blown around takes some concentration, especially if the sail accidentally explodes in your face. With a **bow bag** (p27G), I've found a batten sail can be easily folded in half, and the bottom section securely **tucked under the bag** (E) without straps. Better still, a paddle also jams under there. It's now possible to switch from paddling to sailing or vice versa in just a few seconds. On the water this matters when, despite your best efforts, you find yourself blown towards the shallows and need to drop the sail before switching to paddle-power and steering away.

CRUISING, STEERING & SKEGS

Longer boats work better, but all sailing packrafts will benefit from a **skeg**; the bigger the better. Acting like a trailing keel, you'll be surprised to find you can steer with the control line up to 45° off a tailwind. Some clamp the paddle under an arm to use as a rudder, but even leashed, there can be too much going on managing the sail and paddle. I'd sooner steer with the line (pull left to go left) with the paddle stowed under a bow bag.

In *calmer conditions* **cruise hands-free** by hooking the control line behind your head, clipping it to your PFD or to a longer boat's hull. (Fit an over-long control line to knot shorter, as needed.) Now you can combine paddle power if winds are light, or to warm up as you may miss the body heat generated from paddling. On lively rivers the current and associated entrapments are recognised hazards, but tipped out on a lake, the **wind** can whisk an empty boat out of reach, as widely-used SUP-board leashes testify. A leashed paddle (as well as the loose sail and secured baggage) will slow down a runaway boat.

Caught in squalls gusting up to 30mph, I found my 2.3m packraft surprisingly stable as it got hauled along in 6mph lurches. I put this down to the modest waves at the upwind end of a loch before any 'fetch' had built up, but also a planted feel attributed to in-hull storage. In such conditions **hold the lines in your hands** (D) and be ready to brace against the next squall, because one thing you don't want is to let them slip from cold hands and have the loose sail immediately run over by your charging boat which may slew sideways and eject you. As with whitewater, sailing strong winds is a thrill, but demands your full attention.

PACKRAFTS AT SEA

Britain's 10,000-mile coastline is far more interesting than it's paddleable rivers, but given what we know of waves crashing over lighthouses, it's not surprising most baulk at the idea of paddling a tiny packraft at sea. In fact, **saltwater packrafting** can reveal a new world of nesting sea birds, furtive seals and hidden coves and arches. All you need is good weather and an awareness of your vulnerability in the face of the sea's power. Longer packrafts are faster which can matter at sea, but while fun, **tandem paddling** (A) won't add speed, it just shares the effort.

ABOUT TIDES

Most of us understand the tide comes in and goes out (floods and ebbs) due to the moon's gravity. Enclosed seas like the Mediterranean barely have tides, but the UK definitely does. That's a lot of energy sloshing to and fro every few hours.

Tides don't actually go in and out, but travel along a coast. Around the British Isles a bulge of water rolls in from the Atlantic up the Irish Sea and up the Channel, before swirling round to meet halfway up the east coast.

The cycle from high to low to high is fixed at 12 hours 25 minutes and each day High Water (HW) occurs 54 minutes later. In the UK **tide times** are always in GMT, so in summer (BST) add an hour. For 7-day predictions visit ukho.gov.uk/easytide or bbc.co.uk/weather/coast-and-sea.

RANGE, PHASE & TIDAL RACES

Tidal range is the difference between low and high water and varies by location and day. Britain has among the world's biggest tidal ranges. The shoreline, seabed profile and the surging Atlantic to the west explain why the funnelled Severn estuary has a tide range up to 16 metres. Even the River Thames near London Bridge (B) can exceed 7 metres, and this high range can leave you with a messy, muddy slog if you mistime getting off some of the southwest's many estuaries, or the Wye (C).

The phase of the moon also dictates a cycle of **spring and neap tides.** Occurring a week apart, spring tides rise higher ('spring forth') drop lower, and can increase the daily tidal range by fifty percent: a 4m neap becomes a 6m spring a week later. Because that's a load more water shifting in the same 12 hours 25 minutes, spring tide currents (or 'streams') run faster, especially at mid-tide.

Constrictions accelerate currents, just like a river speeds up though a gorge. Narrow passages from large inlets form **tidal races** with standing waves, eddies and whirlpools on the ebb, as well as unbalancing the flood/ebb cycle. For example Poole Harbour or Loch Etive near Oban take seven hours to fill, but drain in five-and-a-half. At the mouth of Loch Etive the 'Falls of Lora' rise up as the 20-mile-long loch discharges. Other factors can skew a tide table's steady sine wave.

WORKING WITH THE TIDE

Running a river on an ebbing spring tide can be a blast. Battling that same current upstream will be impossible. Just like the weather, tide times are forecasts: usually right but sometimes wrong. Low pressure and strong winds can push high tides higher. Estimating tides at unlisted locations is also tricky; **local knowledge** can help. If you're unsure of a **current's direction**, look for leaning buoys, moored boats or streaming seaweed below you.

Realistically, **day trips** are what's manageable in a packraft, and short ones at that. The **wind** chooses the day and the tide may govern the time. Until you know better, avoid spring tides on exposed shores unless you understand how they can help you on a one-way paddle. Far better to use a packraft to explore intimate nooks and crannies just a short distance from your put-in.

SAFETY AT SEA

Though European countries are stricter and there's talk in the UK of regulating boats over 2.5m (eg. tandem packrafts), in the UK you can sea paddle without a licence or registration. But reconsider the list on p36 and read RNLI pdf: rnli.org/safety/choose-your-activity/kayaking-and-canoeing. It can seem serious and so it is if you don't know when to call it off or turn back. On longer routes identify possible **early take-outs** if things go awry.

The good thing with sea paddling is that, unlike rivers or lakes, most packrafters recognise the commitment needed and approach (or avoid) it accordingly. As with winter hill-walking, ideal conditions for sea packrafting are rare, but with a boat you can deploy in minutes, a sunny, calm day on Britain's wilder shores could provide some memorable packrafting moments (**D**).

PACKRAFTING ADVENTURES

You've got to grips with paddling and equipping your packraft. Now you're ready for a multi-day, self-sufficient adventure out in the wilds. What makes a good packrafting destination? **Follow a river** you might think. But as suggested on p16-19, for more than a day trip that river has to be just right. You can walk your packraft anywhere.

The **Scottish Highlands** pictured widely in this book are Britain's 'mini-Alaska' – a packrafting playground with possibilities limited only by your enthusiasm and, once you get there, the weather. Remembering that you'd rather float, but can walk when you must, it's easy to string together a tide-and-watershed circuit between two parallel west-coast sea lochs, a lap of adjacent freshwater lochs like the Assynt or Rannoch Moor, or an all-out eastbound coast to coast, ending on Goldilocks rivers like the Spey or the Tay to the North Sea.

Unless you're confident, initially **choose a familiar place** where you can visualise packrafting. **Access** also shapes itineraries: where to leave a car and how to get back to it, or public transport, ferries and taxis, and even small planes (A).

These days excellent **mapping resources** include satellite imagery so detailed you can pinpoint rapids and weirs. Drooling over the blue bits on map, it's easy to get over-ambitious. Google is well known, but **Bing Aerial** is often clearer and includes an OS map layer down to 1:25k scale. On nakarte.me you switch between several maps.

The risks are on the water, so closely evaluate all rivers or open crossings, including tide times and phases. If a burn turns out to be a bony trickle, or a loch is streaming with white caps, how feasible is the walk? Jot down the estimated distances of each walking or paddling stage so you know at a glance what you're in for once there. Days spent poring back and forth over your route are never wasted, until it's all embedded in your memory. I'd sooner rely on **paper maps** (or print-outs) and a proper GPS switched on as needed, than smartphone mapping apps like Gaia, even used offline. So get big waterproof mapcase (C).

On land, endeavour to **follow level paths** or tracks. Even if possible, **cross-country** tramping can be exhausting and slow with a full pack. **Trekking poles** help with balance and spreading the load; I prefer my paddle shaft converted to a **packstaff** (B; see website) to probe bogs, vault streams, or balance over stepping stones.

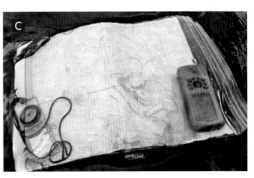

TOO MUCH STUFF

It's normal to pack items 'just in case', particularly for days in the middle of nowhere with the likelihood of poor weather. Weighing your pack then hoisting it on can be shocking, even with several days food. Anything over **16 kilos** (35lbs) will be hard work if there's much hill walking.

Above **D** was the gear carried for the Fitzroy (below). With days up to 40°C we didn't need waterproofs, extra clothing or even sleeping bags, and an inner tent was sufficient, but that same heat added a few virtual kilos.

Note a 5-litre water bag **D1**, waterproof lunch box **2**; water filter **E**, maps, compass and a mini GPS **3**. With less exposed walking than expected, we poked red-hot tent pegs through our GoreTex boots **D4** to enable draining while wading.

A week's food was bagged up into seven Breakfast, Lunch, Dinners **D5**; a better system than just estimating loads of food. Firewood was plentiful and we could roast garlic-oil flatbreads on embers; a delicious antidote to bag food.

With the boat, it all fitted easily in my 90-litre UDB and the yellow Watershed day bag **F**.

FITZROY RIVER, NORTHWEST AUSTRALIA

The Kimberley is Australia's last frontier, a rugged wilderness of marginal cattle stations wracked by wildfires, monsoons and huge tides. I'd gotten to know the area for work, and once I discovered packrafting, it seemed a perfect place for a week's adventure. Even following a river, seven days would be the limit as no matter how easy we made it, the enervating Kimberley would take its toll.

Rivers drain into the Timor Sea, a vast, fjord-riddled coastline with one small settlement. But saltwater crocodiles and heaving, 10-metre tides made bobbing around in an inflatable waiting for a float plane pick-up too sketchy.

We settled on the Fitzroy, 500km inland, securing permission to cross arid station land. We flew from a small town where the river met the highway to a remote camp. Once dropped off at the riverbank, we spent five fabulous days paddling or wading 80 miles back, an adventure only made viable in portable boats.

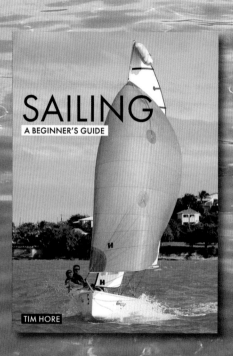
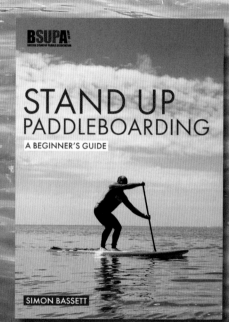
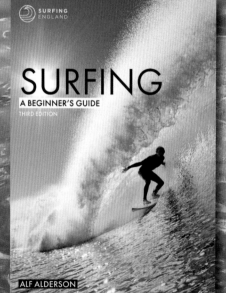
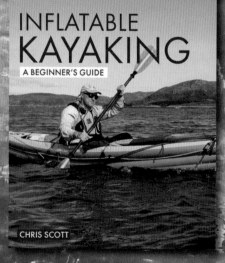